ROMANTIC DINNERS
FOR TWO

Chef Robért Presents

Romantic Dinners For Two

Romp Thru Concepts Inc.
www.rompthruconcepts.com

presents

Romantic Dinners For Two

Library and Archives Canada Cataloguing in Publication

Robért, Chef, 1959-

Chef Robért presents romantic dinners for two.

ISBN 0-9738740-0-7

1. Cookery for two. 2. Menus. I. Title.

II. Title: Romantic dinners for two.

TX652.R622 2006   641.5'612   C2006-901765-4

Food Editor/Chef:	Robért Catherine
Artistic Director:	Barb Catherine
Project Director:	Glenn Froese
Spiritual Advisor:	Wendy Froese
DVD Production:	Canadian Arts Production
Photography:	Trevor Booth Photography
	www.trevorboothphotography.ca
Logo Design:	Bryan Skene
	www.bskene.tradigitalfour.com
Book Design:	Karen Veryle Monck
Printed in China by:	TSE Worldwide Press Inc.

1st Edition 2006
Published by: Romp Thru Concepts Inc.
                       4253 Masotti
                       Windsor, ON Canada N9G 2V4

www.rompthruconcepts.com
www.chefrobertpresents.com
www.romanticdinnersfortwo.com

There is nothing that is a better investment

than your love for each other

and so we encourage you

to turn love into a verb and take action.

Love is the answer. It is magic!

Table of Contents

Table of Contents

Rendezvous Three

Introduction

We would like to thank you for buying our cookbook

Romantic Dinners for Two

Together we are going to show you how to have a truly intimate and memorable dining experience right in your own home.

What an aphrodisiac for your partner to be the guest of honour for a romantic dinner that you took the time to plan and cook.

Being married for 22 years we have shared wonderful romantic evenings together. Robért, being the chef in our home, has made many creative and stimulating romantic dinners. We would like to share some of these recipes and ideas with you.

This DVD shows step by step easy instructions on how to prepare and cook three different romantic dinners.

To help you coordinate the evening we supply you with *Seven Day Planners*, *Invitations*, *Romantic Scenarios*, helpful ideas on *Mood Enhancers* and questions to ask in the *Conversation Ignitors*.

Give yourselves the gift of
Love and Friendship.

Lovingly Chef Robért and Barb

How to Use
the Cookbook and DVD

Chef Robért's *Romantic Dinners for Two DVD and Cookbook* are designed to provide you with easy step by step instructions for each recipe. Open your cookbook and insert the DVD. Using them simultaneously is a recipe for success. So come on, "Let's get cooking".

When a recipe has *"View DVD,"* these are steps that will provide additional professional instructions so you can cook like a chef in your own home. I call these *"Chef Robért Tips."*

This cookbook and DVD are designed to allow for three separate dining occasions. We suggest that one meal is for *you* to prepare for your partner, the other meal is for *your partner* to prepare for you and the third meal is to be enjoyed by preparing it *together*.

When planning your *Romantic Rendezvous* read and review the *Mood Enhancers*, *Romantic Scenarios*, and *Conversation Ignitors*. These will add those extra personal touches and allow you to connect with each other. The *Grocery List* identifies the ingredients you will need for the dinner, along with a *Seven Day Planner* which helps you organize one week before the *Romantic Rendezvous*.

You are now ready to start cooking your dinner.

Each Rendezvous is broken into three sections.

1. **The Ingredients:** The Ingredients section lists the necessary ingredients and outlines preparation time.

2. **Cooking Instructions:** Cooking instructions give you simple detailed instructions on preparing your dinner.

3. **The Final Preparation and Serving Schedule:** The Final Preparation and Serving Schedule guides you through the final touches with each meal allowing you to be a Professional Chef right in your own home.

Let's Get Cooking!

Romantic Scenarios

Scenarios are part of having a truly romantic experience.

We share with you three romantic scenarios to make your dinners sparkle with ambiance. An intimate dining room, cozy fireplace and a sensuous bedroom setting help you create the background for a beautiful evening together.

The DVD shows detailed instructions on each scenario.

Once in a while, right in the middle of life, love gives us a fairytale.

Rendezvous One

You are invited
to a Romantic Rendezvous

Prepared With Love Especially For

_____

Dinner will be served on this day

_____

at _____ *o'clock, in the* _____

Please dress in _____ *attire.*

Special Instructions _____

_____

With love ,

_____

Menu

Passionate Tortellini

Spinach Salad with Warm Bacon Dressing

Chicken à la Chef Robért

Roasted Potatoes and Seasoned Baby Carrots

Chocolate Mousse

How to Use
the Conversation Ignitors

The purpose is to stimulate conversation between the two of you.

Conversation Ignitors are to be used during your Romantic Dinner
in the following ways.

♥ You can be the partner asking all the questions during dinner.
or

♥ You can cut each question out and put them in a fancy bowl.
During the dinner you and your partner will take turns
choosing a question to ask each other.

Remember the LOVE code.
Women like it slow, men are fast.
Women are auditory, tell her.
Men are visual, show him.

Conversation Ignitors

♥ Who has been the most influential person in your life?

- -

♥ What are your goals in the near future?

- -

♥ If you could do it all over again what career/life choices
would you do differently?

- -

♥ What has been your most life altering event?

- -

♥ What is your fondest memory during our time together?

Grocery & Tools List

DAIRY/ EGGS

4 eggs
250 g cream cheese
500 ml/ 16 oz. 35% cream
125 ml/ 4 oz. milk
250 g/ 4 oz. shredded medium cheddar cheese
5 Tbsp. parmesan cheese
3 Tbsp. salted butter

BAKING GOODS

2 Tbsp. icing sugar
7 Tbsp. white sugar
1/4 Tsp. cream of tartar
1/4 cup salt
1 oz. or (block) bitter sweet chocolate
1/4 cup white chocolate chips
1/4 cup all purpose flour

SPICES/FLAVOURINGS

3 Tbsp. seasoning salt
3 Tbsp. pepper
1/4 Tsp. Worcestershire sauce

OILS/ VINEGARS

1 cup olive oil
1/2 cup red wine vinegar

PRODUCE

2 cups fresh spinach
5 fresh white mushrooms
1 red onion
1 small pkg. alfalfa sprouts
5 green onions
2 fresh strawberries
12 baby carrots
4 small whole red potatoes
1 carrot
1 pkg. fresh sage
1 bunch fresh parsley

MEAT

2 (250g-350g/8-10 oz.) boneless skinless
   chicken breasts
4 slices bacon
3 thin slices prosciutto

SPECIALTY ITEMS

2 chocolate coated wafer rolls
500g/ 16 oz. bread crumbs
350 g/ 12 oz. fresh tri-coloured meat filled
        tortellini

TOOLS AND EQUIPMENT

hand mixer or table top mixer	Chef's knife or French knife	3 rectangular containers
medium bowls	paring knife	baking dishes
microwaveable bowls	frying pans	tongs
tablespoons	saucepans	colander
teaspoons	8 serving plates	1 vegetable peeler
rubber spatulas	cutting board	2 wine glasses
	wooden spoons	

Seven-Day Planner

♥ Day 1

Note:

I have set aside Day 5 and Day 6 for cooking. This will allow you to have more spare time on your Romantic Day. If you want, you can prepare everything on Day 7, but you need to allow 4 hours of cooking time and preparation. I recommend following the *Seven Day Planner* for the best results.

Read *Rendezvous One* and review DVD.

Give your partner the invitation.

Plan for privacy. That means if you have children make arrangements for an overnight stay.

♥ Day 2

Select a suggestion from the *Mood Enhancers* and take action.

♥ Day 3

Use the grocery list provided in *Rendezvous One* and go shopping.

♥ Day 4

Plan and create your *Romantic Scenario*. Remember, use items you already have in your home. Purchase anything that will add to your evening. **Candles, Candles, Candles,** you can never have enough!

♥ Day 5

Prepare Chocolate Mousse.

♥ Day 6

Prepare Spinach Salad with Warm Bacon Dressing.

Prepare Chicken à la Chef Robért.

Prepare carrots.

Prepare Tortellini.

Decide what you are going to wear.

♥ Day 7

Set your *Romantic Scenario*.

Review the *Final Preparation and Serving Schedule* so you can cook the food according to the time your Romantic Dinner will be served.

Important! Whatever time you planned for your romantic dinner you must start the *Final Preparation and Serving Schedule* 50 minutes before your dinner.

Rendezvous One Menu

Chocolate Mousse

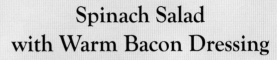

Spinach Salad
with Warm Bacon Dressing

Chicken à la Chef Robért

Passionate Tortellini

Chocolate Mousse

Preparation Time: 1 hour

Tbsp. = Tablespoon
Tsp. = Teaspoon

Ingredients needed for each step:

♥ Step # 1

2   eggs (save egg yolks for Chicken à la Chef Robért recipe)
1   pkg. cream cheese

♥ Step # 2

1 oz.   (block) bitter sweet chocolate
1/4   cup white chocolate
1/2   cup whipping cream in separate
    bowls (1/4 cup in each bowl)

♥ Step # 3

ingredients from previous steps

♥ Step # 4

2   egg whites
2   Tbsp. icing sugar
2   Tbsp. white sugar
1/4   Tsp. cream tartar

♥ Step # 5

1/2   cup cream cheese

♥ Step # 6, 7, 8

ingredients from previous steps

♥ Final Touches *(See Final Preparation and Serving Schedule)*

2   fresh strawberries
2   chocolate wafer rolls

Mood Enhancers

♥ *Be Rested*
♥ *Serve Wine or an Alcoholic Beverage with Your Meal*

Cooking Instructions (View DVD)

♥ Step # 1: Egg Whites and Cream Cheese Preparation
Materials needed: 1 medium bowl, 2 small bowls

> TAKE CREAM CHEESE FROM THE REFRIGERATOR AND ALLOW TO SOFTEN AT ROOM TEMPERATURE.
>
> Take 2 eggs and separate the yolk from the egg whites using 2 small bowls.
>
> **Save egg yolks for Chicken à la Chef Robért recipe.**
>
> Place the egg whites in a medium bowl and allow the whites to sit at room temperature for 30 minutes.
>
> This must be done before starting Step #2. Use this time to assemble and organize cooking tools and ingredients.

♥ Step # 2: Chocolates and Whipping Cream
Materials needed: 2 small microwaveable bowls

> In the first microwaveable bowl add 1/4 cup whipping cream and 1 block (1 oz.) bittersweet chocolate.
>
> In the second microwaveable bowl add 1/4 cup whipping cream and 1/4 cup white chocolate.
>
> **If NO MICROWAVE, heat cream and chocolate on low heat in a small saucepan until chocolate is melted.**

♥ Step # 3: Preparing Chocolates and Whipping Cream
Materials needed: 2 teaspoons

> Place both bowls in the microwave on high for 2 minutes. **Make sure chocolate is melted.** Place the 2 bowls at your work area and using separate teaspoons mix each individual chocolate and whipping cream mixture together so there are no lumps.
>
> Refrigerate.

♥ Step # 4: Preparing Egg Whites
Materials needed: medium size mixing bowl, mixer, spatula, plastic wrap

> Add to mixing bowl, 2 egg whites, 2 Tbsp. white sugar, 2 Tbsp. icing sugar and 1/4 tsp. cream of tartar. Using a mixer, mix on high speed for 10 minutes until fluffy. Cover with plastic wrap. Refrigerate.

♥ Step # 5: Preparing Cream Cheese
Materials needed: 2 medium mixing bowls, mixer, spatula

> In a medium size mixing bowl add 1/2 cup cream cheese. Using a mixer, mix on high speed for 4 minutes. Leave half of the cream cheese in the mixing bowl. Place the other half in another mixing bowl.

♥ Step # 6: Mixing Together
Materials needed: hand mixer, the 2 chocolate and whipping cream mixtures
(refrigerator) and the 2 cream cheese mixtures, 1 spatula

Place the white chocolate/whipping cream mixture in one of the cream cheese mixtures. Mix at high speed for 3 minutes, until fluffy and thick. Add the dark chocolate/whipping cream mixture to the other remaining cream cheese mixture. Mix at high speed for 3 minutes until fluffy and thick.

♥ Step # 7: Making Chocolate Mousse
Materials needed: white and chocolate cream cheese mixture, egg white mixture
(refrigerator), 2 spatulas

Divide the whipped egg whites equally in half and place one half into the dark chocolate cream cheese mixture and the other half into the white chocolate cream cheese mixture.

Using a spatula fold together the egg whites and dark chocolate cream cheese mixture until the egg whites turn the chocolate colour. Using a spatula, fold the egg whites with the white chocolate cream cheese mixture until the egg whites turn the same colour of the white chocolate.

♥ Step # 8: Filling Wine Glasses
Materials needed: white and dark chocolate mousse, 2 wine glasses, 4 teaspoons

Using a teaspoon, scoop a little of the white mousse, carefully allow the white mousse to fall into the wine glass. **Using another teaspoon push the mousse off the teaspoon.** Using another teaspoon scoop up a little dark chocolate mousse and place it over the wine glass, allow the chocolate mousse to fall on top of the white mousse. Repeat these steps until you have filled the wine glass with white and chocolate mousse layers. Repeat with the second glass. Refrigerate

When you are ready to begin serving your romantic dinner go to the
Final Preparation and Serving Schedule for the finishing touches.
Rendezvous One page # 41

Great job !
Now it is time to clean up and get ready for the next course.

Spinach Salad
with
Warm Bacon Dressing

Preparation Time: 30 Minutes
Wash Vegetables

Tbsp. = Tablespoon
Tsp. = Teaspoon

Ingredients needed for each step:

♥ **Step # 1**

4	slices bacon

♥ **Step # 2**

1/4	cup olive oil
1/2	cup red wine vinegar
5	Tbsp. white sugar
1	pinch salt
1	pinch pepper

♥ **Step # 3**

2	cups fresh spinach
3	fresh whole mushrooms (sliced thinly)
1/4	red onion (sliced thinly)
1/2	cup alfalfa sprouts

Mood Enhancer
♥ *On your invitation you can add extra instructions to personalize your evening —eg. give your partner a gift certificate to a spa, or a specific dress attire for the Rendezvous*

Cooking Instructions

♥ **Step # 1: Chopping bacon**
Materials needed: Chef's knife/French knife, plate, cutting board

    Chop bacon into 1/4 inch pieces.

    Place on a plate.

♥ **Step # 2: Warm Bacon Dressing**
Materials needed: frying pan, wooden spoon, medium microwavable bowl, plastic wrap

    Place frying pan on a stove top burner and turn to medium heat.

    Add your chopped bacon to the frying pan and cook until crispy.

    This should take about 3-5 minutes.

    Stir occasionally.

    DO NOT REMOVE OR DISCARD THE BACON OIL, THIS ADDS FLAVOR.

    When the bacon is nice and crisp continue cooking on medium heat.

    Add 1/4 cup of olive oil, 1/2 cup of red wine vinegar, 5 Tbsp of white sugar,

    1 pinch of salt and 1 pinch of pepper.

    Mix together and bring to a boil, stirring occasionally.

    When the bacon dressing comes to a boil remove from the stove top. Shut off burner and carefully pour warm bacon dressing into a microwaveable bowl.

    Cover the bowl with plastic wrap. Refrigerate.

♥ **Step # 3: Preparing Salad**
Materials needed: 2 plates, plastic wrap

    Place 1 cup of spinach on each plate.

    Divide sliced mushrooms in half and place on top of the spinach.

    Divide red onions in half and place on top of the mushrooms and spinach.

    Divide alpha sprouts in half and place on top of the spinach.

    Cover with plastic wrap. Refrigerate.

Great job !
Now it is time to clean up and get ready for the next course.

When you are ready to begin serving your romantic dinner go to the
Final Preparation and Serving Schedule for the finishing touches.
Rendezvous One page # 41

Notes

Chicken à la Chef Robért

Preparation Time: 35 minutes
Wash Vegetables

Tbsp. = Tablespoon
Tsp. = Teaspoon

Ingredients needed for each step:

♥ Step # 1

3	green onions (remove root ends, chopped)
2	fresh whole mushrooms (finely chopped)
1	Tbsp. olive oil
1/4	Tsp. Worcestershire sauce
1/2	cup of shredded cheddar cheese

♥ Step # 2

2	(8-10 oz.) boneless skinless chicken breasts

♥ Step # 3

1	pinch salt
1	pinch pepper

♥ Step # 4

1/4	cup all purpose flour
2	cups bread crumbs
2	egg yolks
1/2	cup milk
2	Tbsp. seasoning salt
1	Tsp. pepper
1	Tsp. salt

Mood Enhancer

♥ *Buy something sexy to wear for your significant other.*

♥ Step # 5

1/2	cup olive oil

♥ Final Touches (*See Final Preparation and Serving Schedule*)

2	green onions
1	peeled carrot

Cooking Instructions

♥ **Step # 1: Chef Robért's Stuffing**

Materials needed: 1 large frying pan, wooden spoon, medium bowl, plastic wrap

Place a large frying pan on a stove top burner and set to medium heat.

Allow the pan to heat up for **30 seconds.**

Add 1 Tbsp. olive oil, 3 chopped green onions and 2 finely chopped whole mushrooms.

Cook for 5 minutes, stirring occasionally.

Add to the frying pan 1/2 cup of shredded cheddar cheese, and 1/4 Tsp. Worcestershire sauce.

Turn off the burner and remove from heat.

Mix together with a wooden spoon until the cheese has melted.

Done!

Remove the frying pan from the stove top and pour cheddar cheese stuffing into a bowl.

Cover with plastic wrap. Refrigerate.

♥ **Step # 2: Fillet Chicken (View DVD)**

Materials needed: paring knife, cutting board

Lay the chicken breasts smooth side down on a cutting board.

Using a paring knife, cut the breasts horizontally cutting a little more than 3/4 way through.

Do not cut the chicken breasts completely in half.

Fold over the top half of the chicken breasts.

♥ **Step # 3: Stuffing Chicken**

Materials needed: Chef Robért's Cheese Stuffing mix from step #1, two chicken breasts

Fold over both of the chicken breasts, season the inside of the breasts with salt and pepper.

Divide the stuffing in half and stuff both chicken breasts equally.

Fold breasts over stuffing, make sure the chicken breasts completely cover the stuffing.

♥ **Step # 4: Breading (View DVD)**

Materials needed: baking dish, cooking spray, 2 rectangular containers or 2 large plates, fork, medium bowl

Take 1/4 cup of all purpose flour and dump it into one of the rectangular containers. Add to flour, 2 Tsp. seasoning salt, 1 Tsp. pepper, 1 Tsp. salt.

Prepare egg wash

In a mixing bowl, add 2 egg yolks and 1/4 cup milk. Using a whisk, mix together the eggs and milk and pour it into the medium bowl.

Bread Crumb Mixture

In the rectangular container add 2 cups bread crumbs.

Spray baking dish with non-stick cooking spray.
Moving left to right, place your containers on your work area in this order.

1. Stuffed chicken breasts.
2. Flour mixture.
3. Egg wash.
4. Bread crumbs.
5. Baking dish.

Be careful when handling the chicken breasts, try not to let the cheddar cheese stuffing leak out.

Breading the Chicken with Chef Robért Cheese Stuffing
1. Place cheddar stuffed chicken breast in the flour and completely cover it. Remove.
2. Put chicken breast in the egg wash and completely cover it. Remove.
3. Place chicken breast in bread crumb mixture, completely cover and press bread crumbs onto chicken. Repeat steps 1 and 2. **Double breading.**
4. Place in a baking dish.
Do not cover chicken breasts with anything, the breading will fall off the chicken breasts.

♥ **Step # 5: Browning Chicken Breasts**
Materials needed: Large frying pan, 1 pair tongs, 1 baking dish

Remember you are not cooking the chicken you are just browning them.

Add 1/2 cup olive oil to a frying pan, turn a stove top burner to medium heat for 1 minute.

Place breaded chicken breasts in a frying pan and brown on each side for 1-2 minutes.

Remove and place in a baking dish.

♥ **Step # 6: Garnish Green Onion/Carrot (View DVD)**
Materials needed: Paring knife, cutting board, medium bowl, vegetable peeler

Great job !
Now it is time to clean up and get ready for the next course.

When you are ready to begin serving your romantic dinner go to the
Final Preparation and Serving Schedule for the finishing touches.
Rendezvous One page # 41

Passionate Tortellini

Preparation Time: 1 hour
Wash Vegetables

Tbsp. = Tablespoon
Tsp. = Teaspoon

Ingredients needed for each step:

♥ Step # 1

1	12 oz. package of fresh tri-coloured meat filled tortellini
2	Tbsp. salt

♥ Step # 2

4	thin slices of prosciutto (chopped fine)
1	Tbsp. olive oil
1	Tbsp. chopped garlic
2	cups 35% cream

♥ Step # 3

5	Tbsp. of parmesan cheese
1	pinch of pepper
3	Tbsp. of finely chopped parsley

♥ Final Touches *(See Final Preparation and Serving Schedule)*

2	sprigs of parsley

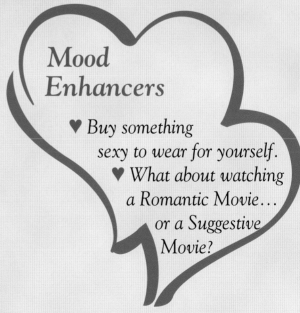

Mood Enhancers

♥ *Buy something sexy to wear for yourself.*
♥ *What about watching a Romantic Movie… or a Suggestive Movie?*

Cooking Instructions

♥ **Step # 1: Preparing Tortellini**
Materials needed: medium bowl, medium saucepan, colander and plastic wrap

Fill a medium saucepan with warm water.

Place a lid on the saucepan bring the water to a boil.

When the water is boiling, use an oven mitt to remove the lid from the saucepan.

Add 2 Tbsp. of salt, 16 oz. of tortellini and let boil uncovered for 5 minutes.

When tortellini is done cooking, remove from the stove top and drain into a colander.

Slowly run cold water into the colander until the tortellini is cold.

Place in a bowl , cover with plastic wrap. Refrigerate.

♥ **Step # 2: Preparing Sauce**
Materials needed: frying pan, wooden spoon

Place frying pan on a stove top burner, set to medium heat and allow frying pan to heat up for 30 seconds.

Add finely chopped prosciutto, 1 Tbsp. olive oil and 1 Tbsp. chopped garlic.

Cook at medium heat for 2 minutes, stirring occasionally.

Add 2 cups 35% cream to the frying pan.

Turn the heat to high and bring sauce to a boil. **Pay attention so the sauce does not boil over.**

When the sauce is boiling, turn down to low heat and cook for 2 minutes.

♥ **Step # 3: Preparing Sauce**
Materials needed: bowl, plastic wrap

After you have cooked your sauce for 2 minutes on low heat, add 5 Tbsp. of parmesan cheese, a pinch of pepper and 3 Tbsp. finely chopped parsley.

Turn heat to high and stir sauce until it comes to a boil, remove the saucepan from stove top and pour the sauce into a bowl.

Cover with plastic wrap. Refrigerate.

Great job !
Now it is time to clean up and get ready for the next course.

When you are ready to begin serving your romantic dinner go to the
Final Preparation and Serving Schedule for the finishing touches.
Rendezvous One page # 41

Braised Baby Carrots
& Seasoned Butter
And Roasted Red Potatoes

Preparation Time: 35 minutes
Wash Vegetables

Tbsp. = Tablespoon
Tsp. = Teaspoon

Ingredients needed for each step:

♥ Step # 1

12	baby carrots
1	pinch of salt

♥ Step # 2

4	small whole red potatoes
4	Tbsp. olive oil
1	Tsp. seasoning salt

♥ Final Touches *(See Final Preparation and Serving Schedule)*

1	pinch pepper
1	pinch seasoning salt
3	Tbsp. butter
1	Tbsp. finely chopped parsley

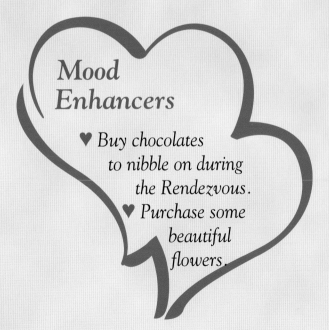

*Mood
Enhancers*

♥ *Buy chocolates
to nibble on during
the Rendezvous.*
♥ *Purchase some
beautiful
flowers.*

Cooking Instructions

♥ **Step # 1: Cooking Carrots**

   Materials needed: small saucepan, colander, small bowl

   Place small saucepan filled with 3/4 cup of water on a stove top burner.

   Set burner to high heat, add 1 pinch of salt, cover pot with a lid, bring water to a boil.

   When the water has boiled, remove the lid, add 12 carrots, boil for 8 minutes uncovered.

   If you like your carrots tender cook 4 minutes longer.

   When the carrots are done, pour the carrots into a colander and run cold water over them for 1 minute.

   Drain. Put the carrots into a bowl.

   Cover with plastic wrap. Refrigerate.

♥ **Step # 2: Roasted Red Potatoes**

   Materials needed: 2 medium bowls, paring knife, baking dish, whisk

   Place 4 red potatoes on your work area.

   Using a paring knife, partially peel off the potato skin from the middle section of the potato. Peel off 1 inch in width in the middle and leave the ends of the potato covered with skin.

   Put the peeled potatoes in a medium bowl with cold water.

   In a medium bowl add 4 Tbsp. olive oil, 1 Tsp. seasoning salt, mix together using a whisk.

   Add the peeled potatoes to the bowl with the seasoning salt and olive oil.

   Toss the potatoes ensuring that all the potatoes are covered with olive oil and seasoning salt.

   Place the potatoes in a baking dish. Refrigerate.

When you are ready to begin serving your romantic dinner go to the
Final Preparation and Serving Schedule **for the finishing touches.**
Rendezvous One **page # 41**

Final Preparation and Serving Schedule
Rendezvous One

Important! Before you start you are going to need two oven racks.

Pre-heat oven to 350° F.

The *Final Preparation and Serving Schedule* is a guide to help you cook and serve your dinner so your food is done on time.

All the courses are prepared and in the refrigerator ready to cook.

Now it's time to follow the final steps to cook your dinner and add your finishing touches.

Important! Whatever time you planned for your romantic dinner you must start cooking 40 minutes before your dinner.

Serve the courses in this order.
1. Passionate Tortellini
2. Spinach Salad
3. Chicken à la Chef Robért with Braised Baby Carrots & Seasoned Butter and Roasted Red Potatoes
4. Chocolate Mousse

♥ Step # 1: Roasted Red Potatoes
1. Place the baking dish with the seasoned and oiled potatoes in the oven on the top rack.
2. Cook at 350° F for 40 minutes.
3. Set timer for 10 minutes so you can place the chicken in the oven when the timer goes off.

♥ Step # 2: Chicken à la Chef Robért
Now that 10 minutes have passed, place the stuffed chicken on the bottom rack and continue to cook at 350° F for the remaining 30 minutes. Re-set timer for 30 minutes. The potatoes and chicken will be done at the same time.

At this time you just finished putting the chicken in the oven. You have 30 minutes before you start your dinner. This is a good time to tidy up or get your evening attire on.

♥ Step # 3: Warming
The oven timer just went off and you are 10 minutes away from dinner. The potatoes and chicken are done. Leave the potatoes and the chicken in the oven and turn down the temperature to 180° F. This will keep the food hot.

For the next two steps you will be using the stove top. You might want to put on an apron so you don't spill anything on your evening attire.

♥ Step # 4: Tortellini

Materials needed: colander, spatula, wooden spoon, frying pan, 2 plates

1. Take your tortellini and sauce out of the refrigerator.
2. Place tortellini into a colander. Run hot water over the tortellini and drain. Place in a bowl.
3. Place the sauce in a frying pan and place on a burner, set heat on medium and cook for 2 minutes.
4. Add your tortellini to the sauce, mix and bring to a boil. Stir occasionally.
5. When the sauce comes to a boil turn off the burner and remove from heat.
6. Plate and garnish.
7. Remember, use your *Conversation Ignitors*.

♥ Step # 5: Salads

Materials needed: 1 tablespoon

1. Remove salads from refrigerator.
2. Place the bowl of bacon dressing in the microwave and set on high, cook for 2 minutes.
3. Stir the bacon dressing with a spoon, pour it equally onto the salads.
4. Serve and give your partner a kiss.

Garnish with fresh sage if available.

♥ Step # 6: Carrots

Materials needed: colander, frying pan, tablespoon, wooden spoon

1. Take the bowl of carrots out of the refrigerator, and place into the sink.
2. Place your bowl under the faucet and slowly run hot water into the bowl, for 1 minute.
3. After 1 minute dump the carrots into a colander and drain.
4. Place a frying pan on the stove top and set to medium heat.
5. Melt 3 Tbsp. butter in a frying pan.
6. When the butter has melted add a pinch of seasoning salt, a pinch of pepper and 1 Tbsp. of finely chopped parsley.
7. Add the carrots to the butter mixture and cook for 1 minute. Stirring occasionally.
8. Serve with Chicken à la Chef Robért.

♥ Step # 7: Serve Chicken à la Chef Robért, Potatoes, Carrots

Materials needed: 2 dinner plates, tongs

1. Plate Chicken à la Chef Robért with potatoes and carrots. Garnish with carrot and green onion flowers.

Take your time and enjoy each other's company.

Remember to use your *Conversation Ignitors*.

♥ **Step # 8: Chocolate Mousse**
Materials needed: paring knife, 2 napkins or doilies, 2 small plates
Cut strawberries in half and place on top of mousse. Insert wafer rolls into Chocolate Mousse.

Now that you have wined and dined your partner,
the rest of the evening is left up to your imagination.

Mood
Enhancers

♥ *Draw a bubble bath*
for your significant other,
either before or after dinner.
♥ *Play soft music*
according to
your taste.

Rendezvous
Two

You are invited
to a Romantic Rendezvous

Prepared With Love Especially For

_____

Dinner will be served on this day

_____

at _____ *o'clock, in the* _____

Please dress in _____ *attire.*

Special Instructions _____

_____

With love ,

_____

Menu
Decadent Nachos
Rings of Love Salad
Beef and Onion Marmalade in Puff Pastry with Asparagus
Cookie Baked Alaska with Raspberry Sauce

How to Use the Conversation Ignitors

The purpose is to stimulate conversation between the two of you.

Conversation Ignitors are to be used during your Romantic Dinner in the following ways.

♥ You can be the partner asking all the questions during dinner.

or

♥ You can cut each question out and put them in a fancy bowl. During the dinner you and your partner will take turns choosing a question to ask each other.

Remember the LOVE code.
Women like it slow, men are fast.
Women are auditory, tell her.
Men are visual, show him.

Conversation Ignitors

♥ Who do you get along with better? Your father or mother?
Why?

- -

♥ If you could change anything in the world,
what would you change?
Why?

- -

♥ Who are the people you depend on?
Who are the people who depend on you?
Who are the people that you think
have made a difference in your life?

- -

♥ What, in your opinion, is the most romantic scenario possible?

- -

♥ If there were any place in the world you could travel
with an unlimited expense account, where would you go?
Why?

Grocery & Tools List

DAIRY/ EGGS
3 large eggs
120 g/ 4 oz. shredded Monterey Jack cheese
250 ml/ 4 oz. sour cream
3 Tbsp. salted butter
1 small pkg. French vanilla ice cream

BAKING GOODS
2 Tbsp. icing sugar
3/4 cup white sugar
4 Tbsp. all purpose flour
1/4 Tsp. cream of tartar
2 Tbsp. salt
4 Tbsp. brown sugar
1 can non-stick cooking spray

SPICES/FLAVOURINGS/JAM
1 Tbsp. vanilla extract
3 Tbsp. currant jelly (red or black)
3 Tbsp. black pepper

OILS/ VINEGARS/WINE
1 cup olive oil
1 cup red wine
1 cup red wine vinegar

PRODUCE
10 asparagus stalks
2 portabella mushrooms
4 whole white mushrooms
1 red pepper
1 green pepper
1 yellow pepper
4 green onions
2 small red onions
1 cooking onion
1 seedless cucumber
1 head Boston bibb lettuce
1 bunch fresh parsley
4 mint leaves
1 small pkg. fresh raspberries
1 bunch fresh Italian parsley
1 pkg. fresh red basil

MEAT
2 (90 g / 3 oz.) beef tenderloin steaks
4 thin slices prosciutto
5 thin slices roast beef deli style

CANNED GOODS
1 can 398 ml / 14 oz. / 19 oz. can sliced beets

SPECIALTY ITEMS
10 large triangle nacho chips
60 ml / 2 oz. salsa
1 small can jalapeño peppers (optional)
1 small jar sliced hot pepper rings
3 small (3 inch) chocolate cookies
3 small (3 inch) oatmeal raisin cookies
1 small pkg. frozen puff pastry
1 small pkg. frozen raspberries

TOOLS AND EQUIPMENT

colander	fork	whisk
frying pan with lid	teaspoons	pastry brush
bowls	hand mixer	cutting board
Chef's knife/French knife	rubber spatula	wooden mixing spoon
saucepan	ice cream scoop	tongs
8 plates	measuring cups	paring knife
baking sheets	measuring spoons	water glass
baking dish	rolling pin	metal spoon

Seven-Day Planner

♥ Day 1

Note:

I have set aside Day 5 and Day 6 for cooking. This will allow you to have more spare time on your Romantic Day. If you want, you can prepare everything on Day 7, but you need to allow 4 hours of cooking time and preparation. I recommend following the *Seven Day Planner* for the best results.

Read *Rendezvous Two* and review DVD.

Give your partner the invitation.

Plan for privacy. That means if you have children make arrangements for an overnight stay.

♥ Day 2

Select a suggestion from the *Mood Enhancers* and take action.

♥ Day 3

Use the grocery list provided in *Rendezvous Two* and go shopping.

♥ Day 4

Plan and create your *Romantic Scenario*. Remember, use items you already have in your home. Purchase anything that will add to your evening. **Candles, Candles, Candles,** you can never have enough!

♥ Day 5

Prepare Cookie Baked Alaska.

Prepare Raspberry Sauce.

Decide what you are going to wear for your *Romantic Rendezvous*.

♥ Day 6

Prepare Beef and Onion Marmalade In Puff Pastry.

Prepare Carrots.

Prepare Rings Of Love Salad.

Prepare vegetables for Decadent Nachoes.

♥ Day 7

Be rested.

Set your *Romantic Scenario*.

Important! Whatever time you planned for your romantic dinner you must start the *Final Preparation and Serving Schedule* 50 minutes before your dinner.

**Baked Cookie Alaska
with Raspberry Sauce**

Rings of Love Salad

**Beef and Onion Marmalade
in Puff Pastry**

Decadent Nachos

Cookie Baked Alaska
with Raspberry Sauce

Preparation Time: 35 Minutes

Tbsp. = Tablespoon
Tsp. = Teaspoon

Ingredients needed for each step:

♥ Step # 1

2	eggs (separate egg whites and use in step #3)

♥ Step # 2

3	chocolate chip cookies (small 3 inches)
3	oatmeal and raisin cookies (small 3 inches)
1	small pkg. vanilla ice cream

♥ Step # 3

2	egg whites
2	Tbsp. icing sugar
1/4	Tsp. cream tartar
2	Tbsp. white sugar

♥ Step # 4

Ingredients from previous steps

♥ Step # 5

2	cups frozen raspberries (defrosted)
1/4	cup white sugar
1	Tbsp. vanilla extract

♥ Final Touches *(See Final Preparation and Serving Schedule)*

1	pkg. fresh raspberries
4	mint leaves

Mood Enhancers
♥ *Write a fantasy for your significant other.*
OR
♥ *Write a poem, love letter, or purchase a card from your local card store.*

Cooking Instructions

♥ **Step # 1: Separate Egg Whites (View DVD)**
Materials needed: 2 small bowls

> Separate 2 egg whites from the yolks and allow to sit at room temperature for 30 minutes. Use in Step #3

♥ **Step # 2: Layering Cookies**
Materials needed: 1 plate, 1 tablespoon

> Take ice cream out of freezer so that it softens. Prepare to layer cookies.
>
> Place an oatmeal cookie on the work counter. Press a 1/2 inch layer of ice cream on top of the cookie, covering it completely.
>
> Place a chocolate chip cookie on the ice cream. Again press a 1/2 inch layer of ice cream on top of the chocolate chip cookie, covering it completely.
>
> Place the oatmeal cookie on top of the ice cream. Done!
>
> Repeat these steps with the other cookies.
>
> Place them on a plate and in the freezer.

♥ **Step # 3: Mixing Egg Whites (Meringue)**
Materials needed: hand mixer, medium bowl

> Place egg whites, 2 Tbsp. white sugar, 1/4 Tsp. cream of tartar, 2 Tbsp. icing sugar into a bowl and mix for 10 minutes.
>
> Mix until firm peaks form.
>
> Tilt the bowl to the side.
>
> If the meringue does not slide, it is done.

♥ **Step # 4: Spread Meringue**
Materials needed: rubber spatula, water glass, baking dish

> Take the layered cookies out of the freezer.
>
> Place the layered cookies on top of a water glass.
>
> Using a cake spatula, spread the meringue all around the sides and tops of the two-layered cookies.
>
> Place in a baking dish.
>
> Put in freezer - DO NOT COVER

♥ **Step # 5: Raspberry Sauce**
Materials needed: wooden spoon, saucepan/frying pan, bowl, fine sieve, metal spoon

Place a saucepan on a stove top burner and set to high heat.

Add 2 cups frozen raspberries with syrup, 1/4 cup white sugar, 1 Tbsp. vanilla extract to the saucepan.

Bring to a boil. Boil for 5 minutes.

Chef Robért Tip: Place a metal spoon in the sauce pan so the sauce does not boil up and overflow.

Mix occasionally.

After boiling for 5 minutes turn the heat down to medium heat.

Cook for another 15 minutes. Mixing occasionally.

Place a fine sieve on top of an empty bowl.

Pour the raspberry sauce into the sieve.

Use a wooden spoon to force the sauce through the sieve into a bowl.

Throw the seeds away.

Place the raspberry sauce in the refrigerator.

Great job !

Now it is time to clean up and get ready for the next course.

When you are ready to begin serving your romantic dinner go to the
Final Preparation and Serving Schedule for the finishing touches.
Rendezvous Two page # 72

Mood
Enhancer
♥ *After dinner,
    give your partner
    a massage.*

Beef and Onion Marmalade in Puff Pastry

Preparation Time: 50 Minutes

Tbsp. = Tablespoon
Tsp. = Teaspoon

Ingredients needed for each step:

♥ Step # 1

1/3	cup olive oil
1	green onion (thinly sliced)
1	cooking onion (thinly sliced)
1/2	red onion (thinly sliced)
3	Tbsp. currant jelly
1	cup dry red wine

♥ Step # 2

2	Tbsp. olive oil
2	(3 oz) beef tenderloin steaks

♥ Step # 3

1	pkg. puff pastry
4	Tbsp. white flour

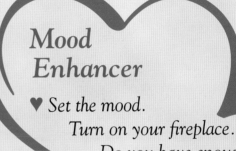

Mood Enhancer

♥ *Set the mood.*
Turn on your fireplace.
— Do you have enough firewood for the evening? Buy a 3-hour log.

♥ Step # 4

2	portabella mushrooms (sliced horizontally)
2	whole white mushrooms (sliced horizontally)
1	pinch salt
1	pinch pepper
2	pieces dried toast cut into circles
1	egg (beaten)
	bowl of onion marmalade mixture

♥ Final Touches *(See Final Preparation and Serving Schedule)*

2	sprigs parsley
4	red basil leaves

Cooking Instructions

♥ **Step # 1: Making Onion Marmalade**
Materials needed: frying pan, wooden spoon, plastic wrap

Place frying pan on a stove top burner and set to medium heat.

Add 1/3 cup olive oil, 1 green onion, 1 cooking onion, 1/2 red onion to the frying pan.

Mix together and cook for 5 minutes, stir occasionally.

Add 1 cup dry red wine and 3 Tbsp. currant jelly to the frying pan.

Continue cooking on medium heat for 25 minutes.

Stirring occasionally, cook until mixture has a thick syrup consistency.

Put in a bowl. Refrigerate.

Cover with plastic wrap. Refrigerate.

♥ **Step # 2: Browning Beef Tenderloin Steaks**
Materials needed: large frying pan, tongs, plate

Put the frying pan on a stove top burner and set to medium heat.

Add 2 Tbsp. olive oil to the frying pan, heat pan for 30 seconds and then add both beef tenderloin steaks to frying pan.

Brown both sides. **If you like your steaks RARE, brown for 30 seconds each side, MEDIUM, 1 minute each side, WELL DONE, 2 minutes each side.**

After browning the steaks remove from the frying pan and place the steaks on a plate to cool.

♥ **Step # 3: Rolling Puff Pastry (View DVD)**
Materials needed: rolling pin

Place 4 Tbsp. white flour on a work area and spread out.

Take half of the package of puff pastry and place it on top of the flour.

Sprinkle small amounts of flour over the pastry so the rolling pin does not stick to the pastry.

Take your rolling pin and roll out one 6-inch square piece of puff pastry. DO NOT ROLL OUT THE PASTRY TOO THIN.
Have at least a 1/8" thickness.

Repeat above steps with other half of the puff pastry.

♥ **Step # 4: Putting it all together (View DVD)**
Materials needed: baking dish, cooking spray, small bowl, teaspoon, pastry brush, paring knife or scissors, tablespoon, fork

Break an egg into a bowl and beat lightly with a fork.

Using a pastry brush, paint a 1 inch edge around the outer edge of the rolled out pastry with the beaten egg mixture.

Place 1 slice portabella mushroom in the middle of the pastry.

Place on top of the portabella mushroom 2 Tbsp. onion marmalade.

Place 1 slice portabella mushroom on the onion marmalade.

Place on top of portabella mushroom 1 Tsp. onion marmalade.

Season beef tenderloin with a pinch of salt and pepper.

Place 1 beef tenderloin on top of onion marmalade.

Add 1 Tsp. onion marmalade.

Add 2 slices whole white mushrooms on top of onion marmalade.

Add 1 tsp. onion marmalade on top of mushrooms.

Place 1 piece dried toast on top of mushrooms. **Toast two pieces of white bread, cut to the size of your beef tenderloin.**

Fold pastry over the ingredients until completely covered. Cut off any excess pastry.

Sprinkle more flour on your work area.

Flip pastry over so the seam is on the bottom, press into the flour, forming a seal.

Using a pastry brush, lightly cover the pastry dough with the beaten egg mixture.

Decorative Touch; Heart on Pastry. (View DVD)

Lightly spray baking dish with cooking spray.

Put the Beef with Onion Marmalade in Puff Pastry in the baking dish.

Repeat above steps for second puff pastry.

Refrigerate.

Great job !
Now it is time to clean up and get ready for the next course.

When you are ready to begin serving your romantic dinner go to the
Final Preparation and Serving Schedule for the finishing touches.
Rendezvous Two page # 72

Rings of Love Salad

Preparation Time: 30 Minutes
Wash vegetables

Tbsp. = Tablespoon
Tsp. = Teaspoon

Ingredients needed for each step:

♥ Step # 1

1	green pepper
1	red pepper
1	yellow pepper
1	head bibb lettuce
1	seedless cucumber
2	whole mushrooms
1/2	red onion

♥ Step # 2

2	green onions (chopped)

♥ Step # 3

4	slices prosciutto (chopped fine)
1/4	cup olive oil

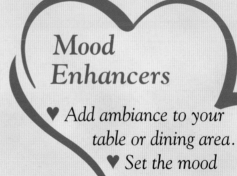

Mood
Enhancers

♥ Add ambiance to your
table or dining area.
♥ Set the mood
with candles.

♥ Step # 4

1	cup red wine vinegar
4	Tbsp. brown sugar
1	pinch salt
1	pinch pepper

♥ Step # 5

	Ingredients used from previous step
1	14 oz. / 19 oz. can sliced beets (including liquid from can)
1	pinch salt
2	pinches pepper

Cooking Instructions

♥ **Step # 1: Preparing Vegetables (View DVD)**
**Materials needed: Chef's knife/French knife, paring knife, cutting board,
4 medium bowls**

> Using a Chef's knife, cut all 3 peppers in half across the width **horizontally**. Remove stem, seeds and white pith.
>
> Take pepper halves and cut the top and bottom from each half, leaving 1/4 inch rings.
>
> Thinly slice 2 mushrooms, cucumber and 1/2 red onion.
>
> Place each vegetable in separate bowls. Set aside.

♥ **Step # 2: Building Rings of Love (View DVD)**
Materials needed: 2 plates, plastic wrap

> Cover 2 plates with bibb lettuce.
>
> Place 3 different coloured rings of peppers on the bibb lettuce. Lay peppers flat so they are not over lapping, all 3 should touch in the middle of the plate.
>
> Build up each pepper ring using cucumbers, mushrooms, red onions and green onions, alternating layering until you use up all the vegetables.
>
> Done! Cover with plastic wrap. Refrigerate

♥ **Step # 3: Salad Dressing**
Materials needed: frying pan, wooden spoon, tablespoon

> Place frying pan on the stove top burner. Set to medium heat.
>
> Add 1/2 cup olive oil, finely chopped prosciutto to the frying pan. Cook 5-10 minutes until prosciutto becomes crispy. Stir occasionally.
>
> Save the oil for the next step!
>
> Using a spoon, remove the prosciutto from the oil. The prosciutto will be used to garnish the salad when serving.

♥ **Step # 4**
Materials needed: frying pan, wooden spoon, medium bowl

> Add to the prosciutto oil, 1 cup red wine vinegar, 4 Tbsp. brown sugar, 1 pinch salt and 1 pinch pepper. Cook in frying pan on medium heat for 2 minutes. Bring to a boil. Remove from heat and place in medium bowl. Allow to cool.

♥ **Step # 5**

Materials needed: blender, 1 bowl, spatula

Pour the ingredients from Step 4 into the blender. Add 1 can sliced beets including juice, 2 pinches pepper, 1 pinch salt.

Using the puree mode, mix in blender for 30 seconds until all ingredients form a creamy consistency.

Refrigerate.

When you are ready to begin serving your romantic dinner go to the
***Final Preparation and Serving Schedule* for the finishing touches.**
Rendezvous Two page # 72

Decadent Nachos

Preparation Time: 20 Minutes   Tbsp. = Tablespoon
Wash Vegetables   Tsp. = Teaspoon

Ingredients needed for each step:

♥ Step # 1

5	slices cooked roast beef (deli style)
1	red pepper
1	green onion
1	yellow pepper
1/4	red onion
1	green pepper

♥ Step # 2

10	large triangular nacho chips
4 oz.	shredded Monterey Jack cheese

♥ Final Touches *(See Final Preparation and Serving Schedule)*

2 oz.	salsa
4 oz.	sour cream
2	Tbsp. jalapeño peppers (optional)
2	Tbsp. hot pepper rings (optional)

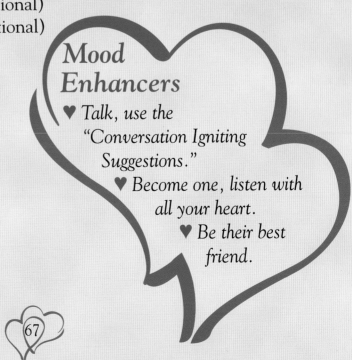

Mood Enhancers
- ♥ *Talk, use the "Conversation Igniting Suggestions."*
- ♥ *Become one, listen with all your heart.*
- ♥ *Be their best friend.*

Cooking Instructions

♥ **Step # 1: Preparation (View DVD)**
Materials needed: Chef's knife/French knife, cutting board, 4 bowls

    Thinly slice red, green and yellow peppers, green onion, 1/4 red onion, place in separate bowls.

    Place roast beef on a cutting board, cut 1 inch squares and place into a bowl.

    Refrigerate.

♥ **Step # 2**

Materials needed: baking sheet, cooking spray

    Lightly spray baking sheet with cooking spray.

    Place 10 nacho chips on a baking sheet. Put 1 piece of roast beef on each nacho chip.

    Sprinkle 1 pinch of Monterey Jack cheese over the roast beef.

    Do not cover. Refrigerate.

When you are ready to begin serving your romantic dinner go to the
***Final Preparation and Serving Schedule* for the finishing touches.**
***Rendezvous Two* page # 72**

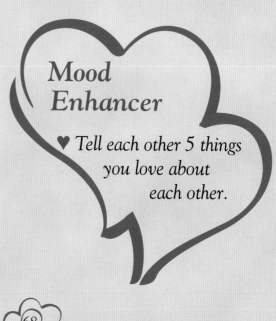

Mood Enhancer

♥ *Tell each other 5 things you love about each other.*

Notes

Asparagus

Preparation Time: 35 Minutes
Wash Vegetables

Tbsp. = Tablespoon
Tsp. = Teaspoon

Ingredients needed for each step:

♥ Step # 1

10	asparagus
1	Tsp. salt
3	Tbsp. butter
1	Tsp. seasoning salt

Mood Enhancer

♥ *Dress up formally*
OR
Have a theme night.

Cooking Instructions

♥ **Step # 1: Preparation**
Materials needed: paring knife, cutting board, 1 bowl
> Cut 3 inches off the bottom of the asparagus.

♥ **Step # 2**
Materials needed: medium saucepan, colander, medium bowl
> Fill saucepan 3/4 full of water, add 1 Tsp. salt and bring to a boil.
> Add asparagus and boil uncovered for 3-5 minutes. Cook until asparagus can bend.
> Remove from heat and run cold water into the saucepan until the asparagus is cold.
> Refrigerate.

When you are ready to begin serving your romantic dinner go to the
Final Preparation and Serving Schedule for the finishing touches.
Rendezvous Two page # 72

Final Preparation and Serving Schedule
Rendezvous Two

Important! Before you start you are going to need two oven racks.

Pre-heat oven to 350° F.

The *Final Preparation and Serving Schedule* is a guide to help you cook and serve your dinner so your food is done on time.

All the courses are prepared and in the refrigerator ready to cook.

Now it's time to follow the final steps to cook your dinner and add your finishing touches.

Important! Whatever time you planned for your romantic dinner you must start cooking 40 minutes before your dinner.

Serve the courses in this order.
> 1. Decadent Nachos
> 2. Rings of Love Salad
> 3. Beef and Onion Marmalade in Puff Pastry with Seasoned Asparagus
> 4. Baked Cookie Alaska with Raspberry Sauce

♥ **Step # 1: Cooking Beef and Onion Marmalade in Puff Pastry**

Place the Beef with Onion Marmalade in Puff Pastry in the oven on the middle rack. Cook at 350°F for 40 minutes. **HOWEVER, SET YOUR TIMER FOR 35 MINUTES SO YOU CAN COOK THE BEEF NACHOS FOR THE <u>LAST 5 MINUTES</u> WITH THE BEEF AND ONION MARMALADE IN PUFF PASTRY.**

♥ **Step # 2: Decadent Nacho Appetizer**
Materials needed: 2 plates, 2 teaspoons

When the timer goes off, place the baking sheet with the beef nachos on the bottom rack of the oven. Set timer for 5 minutes and continue to cook at 350°F.

Have the nacho toppings ready: peppers, onions, sour cream and salsa.

After 5 minutes, take the nachos out from the oven.

TURN OVEN DOWN TO 180°F. LEAVE THE BEEF AND ONION MARMALADE IN PUFF PASTRY IN THE OVEN UNTIL READY TO SERVE.

Place your favourite toppings on the Decadent Nachos.

Plate and serve. **Add some romantic music while enjoying your Nachos.**

♥ **Step # 3: Rings of Love Salad**
Materials needed: 1 ladle

Remove the salad and salad dressing from the refrigerator. Pour 1 full ladle (4 oz.) of salad dressing over each salad. Sprinkle cooked prosciutto bits on top of the salads.

Serve. **When you are finished your salad, take a break and dance with your partner.**

♥ **Step # 4: Beef with Onion Marmalade in Puff Pastry and Seasoned Asparagus**
Materials needed: colander, frying pan, spatula, tongs, 2 plates

Place the bowl of asparagus in the sink. Run hot water over them for 1 minute.

Drain and place in a bowl.

Place a large frying pan on a stove top burner and set to medium heat.

Add 2 Tbsp. butter to the frying pan and add the drained asparagus. Add 1 pinch seasoning salt and cook for 1 minute.

Place the Beef and Onion Marmalade and Asparagus on the plates.

Garnish with red and green basil.

Serve.

♥ **Step # 5: Cookie Baked Alaska**
Materials needed: 2 plates, 1 tablespoon, spatula

Pre-heat oven to 475° F

Take out the Cookie Baked Alaska from the freezer. Place in the oven on the middle rack.

Bake until the meringue is golden.

PAY CLOSE ATTENTION TO THIS. THE MERINGUE WILL BURN.

WHEN THE COOKIE BAKED ALASKA ARE GOLDEN BROWN THEY ARE READY.

Place them on dessert plates.

Take the raspberry sauce out of the refrigerator. Drizzle the sauce around the Baked Cookie Alaska.

DO NOT DRIZZLE SAUCE ON TOP OF THE BAKED COOKIE ALASKA.

Place fresh raspberries on the sauce and serve.

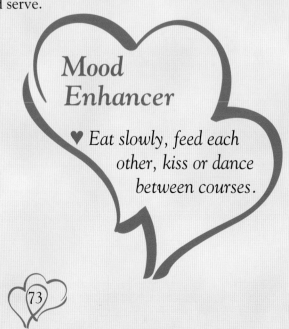

Mood Enhancer

♥ *Eat slowly, feed each other, kiss or dance between courses.*

Rendezvous
Three

How to Use
the Conversation Ignitors

The purpose is to stimulate conversation between the two of you.

Conversation Ignitors are to be used during your Romantic Dinner
in the following ways.

♥ You can be the partner asking all the questions during dinner.

or

♥ You can cut each question out and put them in a fancy bowl.
During the dinner you and your partner will take turns
choosing a question to ask each other.

Remember the LOVE code.
Women like it slow, men are fast.
Women are auditory, tell her.
Men are visual, show him.

Conversation Ignitors

♥ If you could spend 3 months with anyone, dead or alive, who would it be? Why?

- -

♥ If you could spend 6 months with any person, dead or alive, who would it be? Why?

- -

♥ If you could spend 1 year with any person, dead or alive, who would it be? Why?

- -

♥ If there was a super power you could have (i.e. invisible, ESP, fly) what power would you choose? Why?

- -

♥ If there was one famous person in the world you could be, who would it be? Why?

- -

♥ What is the "meaning of life" to you?

Grocery & Tools List

DAIRY/ EGGS
1 large egg
250 g/ 8 oz. salted butter
250 ml/ 8 oz. 35% cream
1 can of ready to use whipping cream

BAKING GOODS
1 cup all purpose flour
2 Tbsp. icing sugar
1/4 cup white sugar
1/4 cup salt
1/2 cup raspberry pie filling

SPICES/FLAVOURINGS
5 Tbsp. black pepper
2 Tbsp. hot sauce

OILS/ VINEGARS/WINE/STOCKS

3/4 cup olive oil
1/2 cup red wine vinegar
1/2 cup white wine
1/2 cup chicken stock

PRODUCE
1 seedless cucumber
1 red pepper
1 yellow pepper

1 red onion
2 fresh white mushrooms
16 cherry tomatoes
2 large tomatoes
1 stalk celery
2 cup salad greens
1 cup fresh spinach
2 cooking onions
1 green onion
1 carrot
1 bunch parsley
6 broccoli florets (one head broccoli)
6 cauliflower florets (one cauliflower)
1 small pkg. fresh raspberries
4 mint leaves
1 Granny Smith apple
2 Tbsp. chopped garlic
1 pkg. fresh rosemary
1 pkg. fresh dill
1 pkg. fresh basil

MEAT

2 (180-240 g / 6-8 oz.) pork chops
8 large cooked shrimp, peeled and deveined

SPECIALTY ITEMS

1/4 cup wild rice blend

TOOLS AND EQUIPMENT		
colander	sieve	2 small plates
hand mixer	paring knife	saucepan
medium size mixing bowl	cutting board	wooden mixing spoon
spatula	French knife/ Chef's knife	large frying pan
2 flan pans	bowls	baking dish
measuring cups	2 small juice glasses	tongs
measuring spoons	or stainless steel tubes	tablespoons
hand grater	whisk	teaspoons
baking sheet/cookie sheet		large serving spoon

Seven-Day Planner

♥ Day 1

Note:

You need to allow 4 hours of preparation and cooking time. Read *Rendezvous Three* and review DVD.

Plan for Privacy. That means if you have children make arrangements for an overnight stay.

♥ Day 2

Each partner picks a suggestion from the *Mood Enhancers* and takes action.

♥ Day 3

Kiss each other passionately for 1 minute. Stop! Don't go any further, let the temperature rise for the romantic day to come.

♥ Day 4

Plan and create your *Romantic Scenario*. Remember, use items you already have in your home. Purchase anything that will add to your evening. **Candles, Candles, Candles,** you can never have enough!

Go grocery shopping together.

♥ Day 5

Again, kiss each other passionately for 1 minute. Stop! Don't go any further. You only have 2 more days until your *Romantic Rendezvous*.

♥ Day 6

Set-up your *Romantic Scenario*.

Decide what you are going to wear.

♥ Day 7

While you are preparing your romantic dinner add music and candles, have a few drinks, dress seductively.

Important! Whatever time you planned for your romantic dinner you must start the *Final Preparation and Serving Schedule* 50 minutes before your dinner.

Raspberry Flan

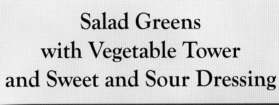

Salad Greens
with Vegetable Tower
and Sweet and Sour Dressing

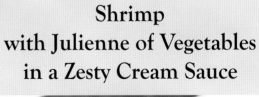

Shrimp
with Julienne of Vegetables
in a Zesty Cream Sauce

Pork Chop
Stuffed with Spinach Apple
and Wild Rice Blend

Raspberry Flan

Preparation Time: 20 Minutes

Tbsp. = Tablespoon
Tsp. = Teaspoon

Ingredients needed for each step:

♥ **Step # 1**

1/4	cup butter (softened)
2	Tbsp. white sugar
1	egg

♥ **Step # 2**

1	cup flour

♥ **Step # 3**

Ingredients from previous steps

♥ **Step # 4**

6	Tbsp. raspberry pie fillings

♥ **Step # 5**

Ingredients from previous steps

♥ **Final Touches** *(See Final Preparation and Serving Schedule)*

2	Tbsp. icing sugar
1	small pkg. fresh raspberries
1	small pkg. fresh mint leaves
1	can whipping cream

Mood Enhancer

♥ *During the week, talk about the up-coming Romantic Rendezvous to increase the suspense.*

Cooking Instructions

Preheat oven to 350°F

♥ **Step # 1: Making Dough (View DVD)**
Materials needed: hand mixer, medium size mixing bowl, spatula

> In a medium size mixing bowl, combine 1/4 cup butter, 1 egg, 2 Tbsp. white sugar.
>
> Using a hand or table top mixer, mix butter, sugar and egg on medium speed for 1 minute.

♥ **Step # 2: Making Dough**
Materials needed: spatula, hand mixer

> Add 1 cup of flour to step # 1 mixture.   Mix together for 30-40 seconds on medium speed.
>
> Using the spatula scrape the excess flour off the sides of the bowl. Mix well.

♥ **Step # 3: Flan Plans**
Materials needed: 2 flan pans, paring knife, cutting board

> Remove the dough from the bowl, form into a ball, flatten and divide into 4 equal pieces.
>
> Take 2 dough pieces, set aside for Step #4. Press remaining dough pieces into each of the flan pans.
>
> Using your fingers, gently press the dough evenly around bottom and sides of the flan pans.

♥ **Step # 4: Raspberry Filling/Shredding dough**
Materials needed: 2 tablespoons, hand grater, cutting board

> Spread 3 Tbsp. raspberry pie filling evenly on top of the dough of each flan.
>
> Using the side of the grater with the largest holes, take 1 piece of dough and shred the dough over your raspberry filling. Shred the dough so it covers the top of the flan evenly.
>
> Repeat with other flan.

♥ **Step # 5: Cooking**
Materials needed: baking sheet / cookie sheet

> Place the raspberry flans on a baking sheet / cookie sheet.
>
> Bake on the middle rack at 350°F for 35 minutes.
>
> Cook until golden brown.

♥ **Final Touches**
See Final Preparation and Serving Schedule

  icing sugar
  fresh raspberries
  fresh mint leaves
  whipping cream

Mood
Enhancer
♥ *Send a love letter*
to your partner
via the mail.

Great job !
Now it is time to clean up and get ready for the next course.

When you are ready to begin serving your romantic dinner go to the
Final Preparation and Serving Schedule for the finishing touches.

Rendezvous Three page # 99

Salad Greens with Vegetable Tower and Sweet and Sour Dressing

Preparation Time: 45 Minutes
Wash Vegetables

Tbsp. = Tablespoon
Tsp. = Teaspoon

Ingredients needed for each step:

♥ Step # 1

1	seedless cucumber
1	red pepper
1	yellow pepper
1	pinch salt

♥ Step # 2

1	Tbsp. olive oil

♥ Step # 3

1/2	cup red wine vinegar
1/4	cup olive oil
3	Tbsp. white sugar
1	pinch salt
1	pinch pepper

♥ Step # 4

Ingredients from previous steps

♥ Step # 5

6	cherry tomatoes
2	cups salad greens
1/4	cup red onions
2	fresh whole mushrooms

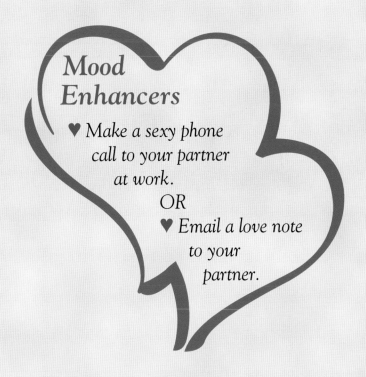

Mood Enhancers
♥ *Make a sexy phone call to your partner at work.*
OR
♥ *Email a love note to your partner.*

Cooking Instructions

♥ **Step # 1: Dicing Vegetables (View DVD)**
Materials needed: 2 cutting boards, 2 Chef knives/French knives, 3 medium bowls, 2 parking knives

Cut cucumber, red and yellow pepper in half. Give half to your partner. Dice vegetables fine.

Keep your vegetables separate from your partners.

Place your vegetables in your bowl.

Mix together and place off to the side.

♥ **Step # 2: Making the Vegetable Towers**
Materials needed: 2 small juice glasses or stainless steel tubes, 2 small plates

Mix vegetables together using your hands. Add 1 pinch of salt.

Using 2 small juice glasses, pour a little amount of olive oil in each glass.

Using your finger smear the insides of the glasses. Pour out any excess oil.

Take the vegetables from the bowls and stuff into the juice glasses.

When stuffing vegetables into the juice glasses, use enough force so that the liquid from the vegetables are removed.

After you have stuffed the glasses, place a small plate over the glass and flip over. Refrigerate.

♥ **Step # 3: Sweet & Sour Dressing**
Materials needed: medium mixing bowl, whisk

Using a medium size mixing bowl add 1/2 cup red wine vinegar, 1/4 cup olive oil,
3 Tbsp. white sugar, 1 pinch salt, 1 pinch pepper.
Mix together using a whisk. Refrigerate.
Remove from the refrigerator 5 minutes before serving.

♥ **Step # 4: Vegetables Towers**
Materials needed: 2 paring knife, 2 salad plates

Take the 2 glasses filled with vegetables out from the refrigerator. Place on your work area.

Using a paring knife, carefully slide the knife around the inside rim of the glass. This will separate the vegetables from the sides of the glass.

Place a salad plate over the glass and firmly hold the plate and glass together. Flip it over.

Holding the plate and glass firmly, shake the plate and glass in a downward motion.
Do this 2-3 times.

Place the plate and glass on the counter.

Slowly lift the glass off the plate, leaving the vegetable tower standing.

Place off to the side.

♥ **Step # 5: Garnish**

Materials needed: 2 cutting boards, 2 Chef's knives/French knives, 2 small bowls

Slice 1/4 red onion very thin. Place in a bowl.

Slice 2 mushrooms very thin. Place in a bowl.

Take your plate with your vegetable tower and place salad greens around the tower.

Sprinkle red onions and mushrooms around the tower.

Place 4 cherry tomatoes on each corner. Refrigerate.

Great job !

Now it is time to clean up and get ready for the next course.

When you are ready to begin serving your romantic dinner go to the
Final Preparation and Serving Schedule **for the finishing touches.**
Rendezvous Three **page # 99**

Mood
Enhancer

♥ *Hide a romanitc gift, give your partner clues to find it.*

Pork Chop Stuffed with Spinach Apple and Wild Rice Blend

Preparation Time: 40 Minutes

Tbsp. = Tablespoon
Tsp. = Teaspoon

Ingredients needed for each step:

♥ Step # 1

1	medium size white onion (chopped fine)
2	Tbsp. olive oil
1/4	cup wild rice blend
1	cup spinach
1/2	cup chicken stock
1	pinch salt
1	pinch pepper

♥ Step # 2

1/2   Granny Smith apple. Remove core.
Leave skin on and chop into medium size pieces.

♥ Step # 3

2   (8-10 oz.) pork chops with bone

♥ Step # 4

1	pinch pepper
1	pinch salt

♥ Step # 5

4	Tbsp. olive oil
1	pinch salt
1	pinch pepper

♥ Step # 6 (View DVD)

2	large tomatoes (for tomato rose garnish)
2	sprigs fresh rosemary

Mood Enhancer

♥ *Write and leave a love note in your partner's car.*

Cooking Instructions

♥ **Step # 1: Stuffing for Pork Chops (View DVD)**
Materials needed: saucepan with a lid, wooden spoon

Place the saucepan on a stove top burner and set to medium heat.

Add 2 Tbsp. olive oil and 1 finely chopped onion. Cook for 2 minutes, stir occasionally.

Add 1/4 cup wild rice to the onion mixture.

Make sure wild rice is mixed well and coated with oil.

Add 1 cup spinach. Mix well.

Add 1/2 cup chicken stock, 1 pinch pepper, 1 pinch salt, mix well.

Put a lid on top of the saucepan and cook on medium heat for 8 minutes. Stir every 2 minutes.

♥ **Step # 2: Adding Apple to Pork Chop Stuffing**
Materials needed: bowl

Add chopped apple to rice and spinach. Mix together.

Turn off the burner, remove the wild rice from the stove top and cover with a lid.

Allow the wild rice and stock mix to cool for 20 minutes.

After 20 minutes place the rice pilaf in a bowl. Refrigerate. Needs to be cooled for the next step.

♥ **Step # 3: Preparing Pork Chops (View DVD)**
Materials needed: 2 paring knives, plate, cutting board

Lay pork chops flat on a cutting board.

Using a paring knife take the pork chops and cut horizontally along the sides of the pork chops, cut 3/4 of the way into the pork chops.

♥ **Step # 4: Stuffing the Pork Chops**
Materials needed: 2 tablespoons, cutting board

Add a pinch of salt and pepper to the inside and outside of the pork chops.

Take half of the cooled rice pilaf and stuff it into the pocket of 1 of the pork chops. Repeat with the other pork chop.

♥ **Step # 5: Browning**
Materials needed: large frying pan, tongs, baking dish

Put a large frying pan on a stove top burner. Set to medium heat, add 4 Tbsp. olive oil, heat for 30 seconds.

Place both stuffed pork chops in the frying pan, brown for 2 minutes on each side. Remember you are not cooking the pork chops just browning them.

Place pork chops in a baking dish. Refrigerate.

♥ Step # 6: Tomato Rose Garnish (View DVD)
   Materials needed: 1 cutting board, 1 paring knife

Great job !
Now it is time to clean up and get ready for the next course.

When you are ready to begin serving your romantic dinner go to the
Final Preparation and Serving Schedule for the finishing touches.
Rendezvous Three page # 99

Broccoli and Cauliflower Florets

Preparation Time: 10 Minutes
Wash Vegetables

Tbsp. = Tablespoon
Tsp. = Teaspoon

Ingredients needed for each step:

♥ **Step # 1**

    2   Tbsp. salt

♥ **Step # 2**

    1   small head of cauliflower **6 florets**
    1   small broccoli **6 florets**

♥ **Final Touches** (*See Final Preparation and Serving Schedule*)

    2   Tbsp. butter
    1   pinch salt
    1   pinch pepper

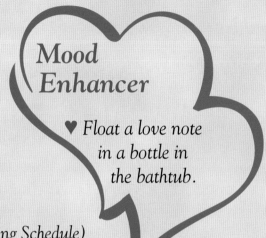

Mood Enhancer

♥ *Float a love note in a bottle in the bathtub.*

Cooking Instructions

♥ **Step # 1: Boiling and cooking vegetables (View DVD)**
Materials needed: medium saucepan, 2 cutting boards, 2 paring knives, 3 medium bowls

    Cut broccoli and cauliflower into florets.

    Medium saucepan, fill 1/2 full of water. Place on a stove top burner and set to high heat.

    Add 2 Tbsp. salt. Bring to a boil.

    Add cauliflower to boiling water. Cook for 2 minutes.

    After 2 minutes add broccoli. Cook for another 4 minutes.

♥ **Step # 2: Drain**
Materials needed: colander, bowl

    Put a colander in the sink, carefully pour cauliflower and broccoli into the colander.

    Immediately run cold water over the vegetables for 2 minutes.

    Place drained vegetables in a bowl. Refrigerate.

♥ **Final Touches** (*See Final Preparation and Serving Schedule*)

Shrimp with Julienne of Vegetables in a Zesty Cream Sauce

Preparation Time: 25 Minutes
Wash Vegetables

Tbsp. = Tablespoon
Tsp. = Teaspoon

Ingredients needed for each step:

♥ Step # 1

1	carrot
1	stalk celery
1/2	white onion
1	green onion
10	cherry tomatoes
1/4	cup fresh parsley

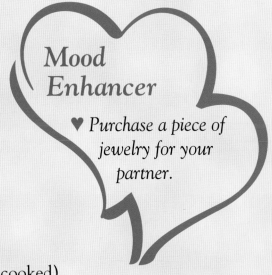

Mood Enhancer

♥ *Purchase a piece of jewelry for your partner.*

♥ Step # 2

2	Tbsp. olive oil
1	Tbsp. garlic (chopped)

♥ Step # 3

8	large shrimp (peeled, deveined and pre-cooked)
1/2	cup white wine
10	cherry tomatoes (cut in half)

♥ Step # 4

1	cup 35 % whipping cream
2	Tbsp. parsley
4	dashes hot sauce
1	pinch salt
1	pinch pepper

♥ Final Touches   (*See Final Preparation and Serving Schedule*)
2	sprigs fresh parsley

Cooking Instructions

♥ **Step # 1: Vegetable Preparation (View DVD)**
Materials needed: 2 bowls, 2 Chef's knives/French knives, 2 cutting boards

    Cut celery, carrot, 1/2 white onion in half and cut very thin (julienne).

    Thinly slice green onion.

    Place cut vegetables in a bowl, set aside for cooking.

    Cut 10 cherry tomatoes in quarters, place in a separate bowl for step #3.

    Chop 1/4 cup fresh parsley. Set aside.

♥ **Step # 2: Cooking Vegetables**
Materials needed: saucepan, wooden spoon

    Put saucepan on a stove top burner and set to medium heat.

    Add 2 Tbsp. olive oil, 1 Tbsp. chopped garlic cook for **30 seconds.**

    Add onions, celery, carrots to saucepan, cook for 5 minutes.

♥ **Step # 3: Adding Wine, Shrimp, Tomatoes**
Materials needed: wooden spoon

    Add 1/2 cup white wine, 8 shrimps, 10 cherry tomatoes to saucepan.

    Cook on medium heat for 8-10 minutes. **Liquid will evaporate.**

♥ **Step # 4: Zesty Cream Sauce**
Materials needed: wooden spoon, medium bowl

    Add 1 cup 35% cream, 4 dashes hot sauce, chopped parsley,

    1 pinch salt, 1 pinch pepper.

    Cook together for 5 minutes.

    Place shrimp and sauce in medium size bowl. Refrigerate.

♥ **Final Touches**
See Final Preparation and Serving Schedule

    2 sprigs fresh dill

When you are ready to begin serving your romantic dinner go to the
Final Preparation and Serving Schedule **for the finishing touches.**
Rendezvous Three **page # 99**

Final Preparation and Serving Schedule
Rendezvous Three

Important! Before you start you are going to need 2 oven racks.

Pre-heat oven to 350°F.

The *Final Preparation and Serving Schedule* is a guide to help you cook and serve your dinner so your food is done on time.

All the courses are prepared and in the refrigerator ready to cook.

Now it's time to follow the final steps to cook your dinner and add your finishing touches.

Important! Whatever time you planned for your romantic dinner you must start cooking 45 minutes before your dinner.

Serve the courses in this order.
1. Shrimp with Julienne of Vegetables in a Zesty Cream Sauce
2. Salad Greens with Vegetable Tower
3. Pork Chops Stuffed with Spinach, Apple and Wild Rice Blend
4. Raspberry Flan

♥ **Step # 1: Cooking Pork Chops Stuffed with Spinach Apple and Wild Rice Blend**

Take the Pork Chops out of the refrigerator and place them on the middle rack in a preheated oven.

Cook at 350°F for 45 minutes. **SET TIMER.**

♥ **Step # 2: Timer**

When the timer goes off, it is time to eat. Turn oven temperature to 180°F. This keeps the pork chops nice and hot. Keep Pork Chops in the oven until you are ready to serve them.

♥ **Step # 3: Shrimp with Julienne of Vegetables in a Zesty Cream Sauce**
Materials needed: 1 tong, wooden spoon, large solid serving spoon

Place saucepan with the **Shrimp with Julienne of Vegetables in a Zesty Cream Sauce** on a burner.

Set heat to medium and bring to a boil, stirring occasionally.

Remove from heat. Divide portions evenly on 2 plates and garnish with fresh dill.

Before you begin to eat your appetizer take the salad dressing out of the refrigerator so it can sit at room temperature.

Toast each other to a memorable evening.

♥ Step # 4: Vegetable Towers with Salad Greens with Sweet and Sour Dressing
Materials needed: 1 tablespoon

Remove **Vegetable Tower with Salad Greens** from the refrigerator.

Pour salad dressing evenly over both salads.

Serve and enjoy!

Present each other with a memorable gift or special card.

♥ Step # 5: Pork Chops with Spinach, Apples with Wild Rice Blend
Materials needed: 2 plates, 1 tong, colander

Take the broccoli and cauliflower out of the refrigerator and place into the sink.

Run hot water over them for 1 minute.

Drain into a colander.

Place vegetables back into a bowl.

Put a medium frying pan on a stove top burner, set to high heat and add 2 Tbsp. butter.

Add the drained vegetables, 1 pinch salt and 1 pinch pepper.

Mix together until butter is melted. Remove from heat.

Remove the pork chops from the oven. Place Pork Chops, Cauliflower and Broccoli on a plate.

Garnish with a tomato rose, basil and rosemary.

Remember to use the *Conversation Ignitors*.

♥ Step # 6: Raspberry Flan
Materials needed: 1 paring knife, 2 plates, tablespoon, small sieve

Place the 2 flans on your work area.

Using a paring knife cut around the inside edge of the flans.

Tip the flan dish over into the palm of your hand releasing the flan into your hand. Place on a plate.

Repeat with the second flan.

Sprinkle with icing sugar, garnish with whipped cream, fresh raspberries and mint leaves.

Remember to have fun and use the *Mood Enhancers*.
Enjoy the rest of your evening.

We Want Your Opinions and Feedback

Complete this questionnaire and send it to Romp Thru Concepts Inc. and you will be automatically registered to win a dinner for four.

Chef Robért will prepare a four course meal right in your own home.

All dinner expenses compliments of Romp Thru Concepts Inc.

No entries will be accepted after December 31, 2007.

Winners will be notified by January 2008. Proof of purchase necessary to win.

Go to page 102 to fill out the questionnaire, or go to

www.romanticdinnersfortwo.com to fill out the on-line questionnaire.

Life is a continual journey of expanding your mind.

Place
stamp
here

Romp Thru Concepts Inc.

4253 Masotti Crest.

Windsor, Ontario

N9G2V4

1. Who purchased the book?   Male _____   Female_____

2. Age group (circle one)   20-29   30-39   40-49   50-59   60-over

3. Marital status: Single_____   Married_____   Other_____

4. Children: Yes_____   No_____

5. Why did you purchase this book?

   Surprise_____   Anniversary_____   Birthday_____   Valentine's Day____

   Wedding Gift_____   Christmas_____   Other_____

6. What did you like about the book? _____

_____

7. What could we improve? _____

_____

8. Would you like to be put on our mailing list?   Yes_____   No_____

9. Did you find the book and DVD easy to follow?   Yes_____   No_____

10. What was your favorite recipe?_____

1. How did you hear about us?   Online_____   Magazine (which one)_____   TV____   Radio____

   Word of Mouth_____   Family or Friend_____   Other_____

12. Any additional comments: _____

_____

Fill out the personal information for your chance to win a dinner for four by Chef Robért:

Name: _____   Email Address: _____

Address:_____

City: _____   State/Province _____   Zip/Postal Code _____

Thank you again

Romp Thru Concepts

A special *Thank You* to the following people who helped and supported us
through our journey in the making of this book.

Gunter and Christa Froese
Darcy Bryn
Tom Smith
Trevor Booth
Pat Jefflyn
Kim Kristy
Karen Veryle Monck
Bryan Skene
Marcie Roselle
Frank Abbruzzese
Ali Jaber

and last, but not least, our families and friends for their patience and encouragement.

Sincerely,

Glenn, Wendy, Barb
and Chef Robért